Read-About® Health

Seeing

By Sharon Gordon

Consultants
Nanci R. Vargus, Ed.D.
Primary Multiage Teacher
Decatur Township Schools, Indianapolis, Indiana

Jan Jenner, Ph.D.

SCHOLASTIC INC.
New York Toronto London Auckland Sydney
Mexico City New Delhi Hong Kong Buenos Aires

Designer: Herman Adler Design
Photo Researcher: Caroline Anderson
The photo on the cover shows a young girl looking in a mirror.

ISBN 0-516-24511-2

12 11 10 9 8 7 6 5 4 3 2 1   2 3 4 5 6 7/0

Printed in the U.S.A.   61

First Scholastic paperback printing, September 2002

Look at that!

4

Your eyes are like cameras that never stop taking pictures.

All day long, your eyes take pictures of the world around you.

Your eyes quickly send
these pictures to your brain.

That is how you see things.

Seeing is one of the five senses. It is called the sense of sight.

The other senses are hearing, touching, smelling, and tasting.

The sense of sight begins with your eyes.

Your eyes are shaped like round balls. You can only see the front of them.

The backs of your eyes are safe inside your head.

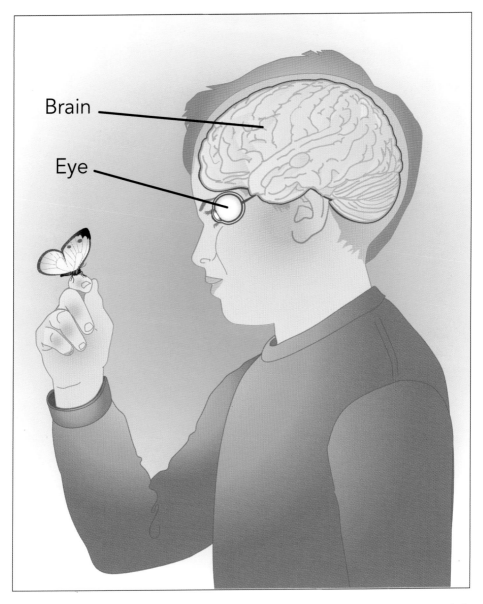

Brain

Eye

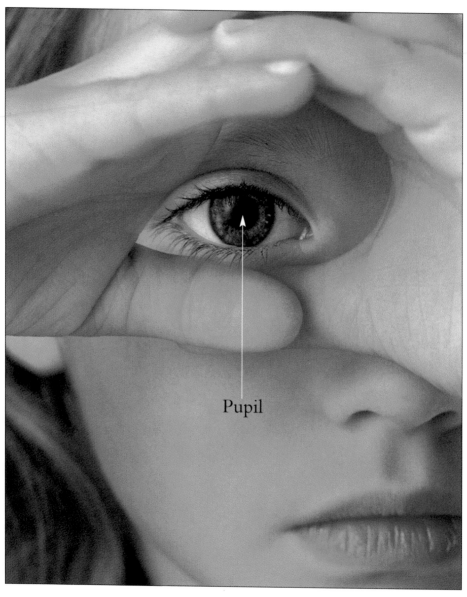

Pupil

Look in a mirror.

The little black circle in the middle of your eye is called the pupil (PYOO-pul). It lets light into your eye.

Iris

The colored part around the pupil is called the iris (EYE-ris).

The iris can be blue, brown, green, or gray. What color eyes do you have?

Iris

The iris has an important job. It changes the size of your pupil to let in more or less light.

Turn on a bright light.

The iris makes your pupil get smaller. It stops too much light from going into your eye.

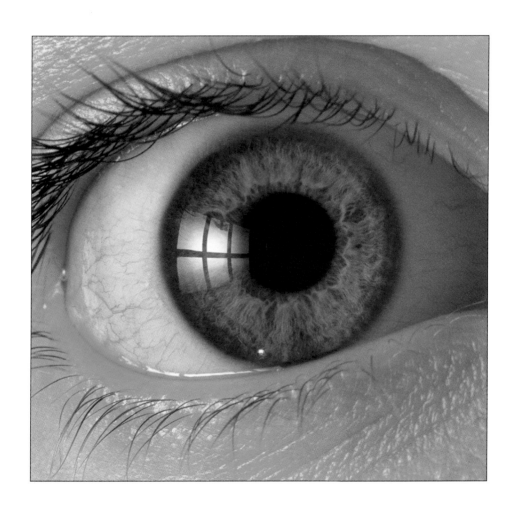

Turn off the light.

Now the iris makes your pupil open wide. Your eye is trying to get in as much light as possible.

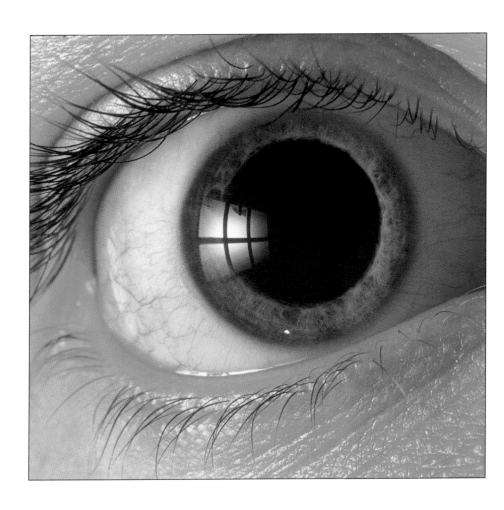

What pictures can you see
with your eyes? You can
see things close to you.
Hello, spider!

You can see things far, far away. Can you count the bright stars?

You can see pretty colors with your eyes. The fall leaves are red and gold.

You can see important shapes with your eyes. Stop!

You can see the words and
pictures in this book.

What are your favorite
things to see?

Words You Know

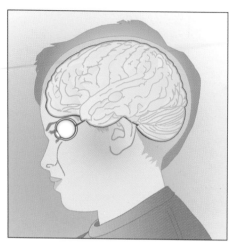

brain

camera

colors

eyes

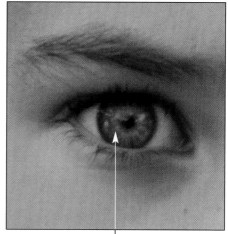

iris

pupil

shape

Index

About the Author

Sharon Gordon is a writer living in Midland Park, New Jersey. She and her husband have three school-aged children and a spoiled pooch. Together they enjoy visiting the Outer Banks of North Carolina as often as possible.

Photo Credits

Photographs ©: Photo Researchers, NY: 14 (Christopher Briscoe), 15, 31 top left (Ken Cavanagh), 3 (Francois Gohier), 19, 21 (Adam Hart-Davis/SPL); PhotoEdit: cover (Myrleen Cate), 7 bottom right (Dennis MacDonald), 7 top left (Alan Oddie); Stone: 27 (Jo Browne/Mick Smee), 29 (Tim Davis), 16, 31 top right (Mark Gervase), 7 top right (Will & Deni McIntyre), 24, 30 bottom (Michael Orton), 22; Superstock, Inc.: 8, 12, 23, 31 bottom left; Viesti Collection, Inc.: 7 bottom left (Martha Cooper), 4, 30 top right (Trina Sustersic), 26, 31 bottom right.

Illustration by Patricia Rasch.